T0194651

# Poems–Puns–Ponderances

### Life, Loss, Love, Laughter–God's Gifts for Healing

E. ROY LAMPINEN

WESTBOW
PRESS®
A DIVISION OF THOMAS NELSON
& ZONDERVAN

WestBow Press books may be ordered through booksellers or by contacting:

WestBow Press
A Division of Thomas Nelson & Zondervan
1663 Liberty Drive
Bloomington, IN 47403
www.westbowpress.com
1 (866) 928-1240

Because of the dynamic nature of the Internet, any web addresses or links contained in this book may have changed since publication and may no longer be valid. The views expressed in this work are solely those of the author and do not necessarily reflect the views of the publisher, and the publisher hereby disclaims any responsibility for them.

Any people depicted in stock imagery provided by Getty Images are models, and such images are being used for illustrative purposes only. Certain stock imagery © Getty Images.

ISBN: 978-1-9736-6583-0 (sc)
ISBN: 978-1-9736-6582-3 (hc)
ISBN: 978-1-9736-6584-7 (e)

Library of Congress Control Number: 2019907582

Print information available on the last page.

WestBow Press rev. date: 6/28/2019

# Contents

## Good Evening, Mr. Frog

Good evening, Mr. Frog.
How do you do?
Can you dance
Like I used to?

I was good in my day.
Why, I could dance in wet clay.

So say, Mr. Frog,
Can you dance upon the pods,
Or do you do it on sand?

Either way, I'd be your fan.
Twould be a thrill to see
You dance upon the pod
Or the sand, Mr. Frog.

Well, goodbye for now; I'll see you later.
I was just out for a stroll.
You see, I can't sleep tonight
As I'm pondering my plight.

Good night, Mr. Frog.
I like where you live.

## Where Are You Tonight, My Dear?

I sit here alone in our living room,
Pondering where you are, my dear.
I thought you'd be home tonight.
I know you took the car.

Oh, where are you tonight, my love?
How can it be that you're not here with me?

Am I supposed to be glad?
Am I supposed to be mad?

I love you so.

Where are you tonight, my dear?
Can you ever leave that cheer?

I love you it's clear.
Oh, where are you tonight, my dear?

Tonight I will hit the hay.
Without you seems the way.

I love you so.

Where are you tonight, my dear?
I guess I lost you long ago.

## Hello, Mr. Mountain

Hello, Mr. Mountain.
How are you today?
Do you have anything to do?
Or are you just that way?

You appear so strong.
Am I wrong?

You are majestic in winter with your white hair.
I like to ski upon you with great dare.

I salute you, Mr. Mountain,
As in spring you are an unselfish fountain.

Your slopes are so clean and fair.
Whenever I hike them up and down,
You take away my frown.

I crave your fresh air.
It is all I declare
When I am there with you.

Thank you, Mr. Mountain, for your
Beauty and esteem; God made you, I know.
And now you give of yourself to me.

## Twas the Night before Wednesday

Twas the night before Wednesday.
And all was so quiet.
It was the pits; I thought it was Friday.

When suddenly there arose such a clatter,
I sprang from my bed and went into
The kitchen to see what was the matter.
And what did my eyes soon see?

Twenty little ants all on the floor,
Just eating and scurrying into the night.
I picked up a damp sponge and headed down.
Wiping each up, I could see the frowns.
I had fun.

I put them into a giant disposal, and away they did swirl.
I could hear each one's scream for help.
I looked around, but no one came.
The poor things died in vain.

And then there was silence, all except for the machine.

Hmm, perhaps I should've left them on the floor
As they were cleaning it all the more.

This all happened because I couldn't sleep.

Being that I am up now, I'll eat a snack.
Maybe then I'll sleep!

## It Is Not Funny Anymore

It is not funny anymore.
I cannot sleep; it's a bore.

What do I do all night long?
If I stay up, is it wrong?

Perhaps as I write I will tire.
I hope I don't set my mind on fire.

It is not funny anymore
As I have work tomorrow galore.
It is just not funny anymore.

Well, maybe if I bang my head against the door ...

(August 10, 2001)

## I Can't Sleep!

Now I would like to lay me down to sleep,
And pray the Lord my soul to keep.
One problem, however—
I can't sleep!

### If I Loved You Any More

If I loved you any more,
I would have to give you my mind, heart, and soul.
If I loved you any more.

If I loved you any more,
I would have to leave my old ways.
If I loved you any more.

I have, and I did
Because I love you even more.

## I Am Angry

I am angry.
My son passed away
Nearly nine months ago, they say.
I don't want to remember that day!

He took his life, you see.
Now, no one he knew is free.

I raise my fist to the skies
And demand that God return him to me
This instant!
With rage, pain, and tears in my eyes,
I say it again!

Then suddenly, I collapse from my vent.
My body grows limp.
I bow my head.
I relent …

He's not coming home.

## He's Never Coming Home

He's never coming home.
I feel so alone.

He left in a hurry—
No notes, no messages.

He didn't take a coat.
Must be warm where he is going.

He fashioned a sheet into a rope,
And then he hung himself.

Without even telling me.
I am angry about that.

I miss him; he was my son.

### Darling, I'm Taking You with Me

Darling, I'm taking you with me as I travel northeast
For it's the thoughts of you that I feast.
N'ermore do I want to be alone in my heart.

Oh, you are wonderful, and you are great.
No man could ask for a more delicious plate.
I love you, I love you.
You, just a sweet thought of the day.

## Dad

Hello, Dad.
It's so good to see you today.
You look as sharp as ever.

This climate must be you
Because it brings out your handsomeness.

Dad, did I tell you I loved you?
Have I told you how grateful I really am for you?

I am, you know,
And that should show.

All those years were not wasted.
They were to help me and my brothers and sister to mellow,
And to try something other than our favorite JELL-O.

You gave us all such a good life,
You and your wife.

We called her Mom, and you called her honey.
You two were in it through thick and thin.
You two were in it for all of us too.

You stayed until her end.
You were brave, and she was grateful.

You are my hero and my friend.
I thank God that you're my dad.
We all do.

## Codependency

I have toiled, it is true,
All my life just for you.

I asked nothing for myself
As I like to give to everyone else.

Life is for giving,
Not receiving.
I had all types of friends then.

They were always around.
Then when it came time to help me,
They were nowhere to be found.

I think it was because they knew
My helping them didn't come from me.
It was from my codependency.

For if I helped them, I must be good.
I must have worth.
For this they had little respect.

They saw through my plight,
My beggar façade.

I wish one of them would've told me.
I might have healed sooner; it's not their fault.

I am codependent today but in a very good way.
And I truly love my friends, and close ones I have.
I am lucky to say
Things are more real, not a charade.

## I Guess He Wanted to Go

I lost a son.
He committed suicide.

He was as bright as the day
And could be as wild as the night.

He loved to dance.
His ambition was to slide across the floor
Like no one before.

We all loved him and told him so.
But that wasn't enough because he decided to go.

He told us many times
That he wanted to die.

We didn't believe him, still the thought made us cry,
Where was the depth of his sorrow, we asked?
He just said he didn't know.

Medication might help, we said,
But he wouldn't consider taking a med.

He must not have liked it here.

We miss him terribly.
He was twenty-two.

## Where Does the Wind Go?

Where does the wind go?
Does anybody know?

When it blows by me,
Why is it in such a hurry?

Does it go all around the earth
And then come back for me to breathe again?

Do others breathe the same wind I do?
Or does it lose its speed and drop to the ground,
And then some new wind starts its round?

Where does that wind go?
Does anybody know?

## I Just Love to Race

I just love to race,
Anywhere, any place.

At the lights or at the track,
It doesn't matter.

I will race a bug
Or a truck carrying a rug.

I will race a Maxima too.
They are easy to chew.

I eat Camaros for lunch
And Firebirds for dinner.
My Aurora is a winner.

Most Mustangs are also soon out of sight.
Their engines are their plight.

Now, I am careful about what I race.
Cobras, Corvettes, Sevilles, and El Dorados—
I stay out of their space,
Else my record would be a disgrace.

At every light there could be a race.
To win another would keep the pace.
Just another notch on the pedal
To win my medal.

I must be careful and watch for the police
Because my fun they would decrease.

I drive an Oldsmobile Aurora,
Quick for a luxury car.
On the road it is a star.

Excuse me, I'm at a light.

### How Does This Happen to Me?

How does this happen to me
When I can't settle down to sleep?

It's been a struggle for too long.
I must see someone to correct this wrong.

Sleep is something we all need.
With this deprivation, I cannot survive.

If somehow I could plant a seed
That it's okay to just lie back,
I might get the sleep I lack.

How does this always happen to me?

## The Airplane at Hancock

I was waiting for my flight.
One came in.
It wasn't mine.

As it readied to leave,
I noticed the propellers
Were not at ease.

They were speeding up in a test,
Making sure they were still the best.

They went faster and faster.
I thought about how quick
You could die jumping into those blades.

One could run out the door and dive into those chewers.
Oh, they were hypnotic.

It would all be over in a split second.
The body would be all over the tarmac.

People would be screaming.
They would be out of control.

All because a man
Wanted to end it all.

Sometimes I feel like that
When my self-worth dwindles.

It's confusing sometimes.
I wonder if anything rhymes.

I do want to stay the course
Until the Lord calls me home.
It will be in His time, not mine.

It was just this thought I wanted to share.
Dying by my hands wouldn't be fair.

## After Lunch

Now it's time to take a nap.
But what about my job?

Oh, forget all that.
My boss won't care.

I don't think he'll give me the electric chair.
I feel like a nap.

I want my way.
Isn't that okay?

But from where is my income derived?
Isn't it how I stay alive?

Oh, boy, I had better go back.
Forget the nap.

I can survive.

Well, it was fun to jump ship
Even for a moment.

My boss will never know
Just how close I came.

To making him the blame
For me being in the unemployment line.

I really do like my job.
Thank God.

## Don't Let It Go to Your Head

I'll tell you something about you.
Just promise not to let it go to you head.

Don't let it go to my head?
Well, what should I do? I'm confused.

Would it be okay to let it go to my feet?
That might be sweet, but what if they smell?

What if I let it go to my knees?
Would that put you out of joint?

Or maybe I can let it go to my throat.
I hope that doesn't make you choke.

What is this phrase that you say?
I have it heard so often
From family and others alike.

You give me this gift
Yet won't let go.

Can I just have what it is you are giving me
And let it go to my head, my knees, or my throat?

To do with it what I please
Since it's a gift you're giving to me?

Or do you insist on this petty control?
If that's the case, thanks.

I think I'll take a stroll.

## My Date

I'm with my date
At her house.
Her sister is with us on the couch.
Her mother is with us too,
Sitting in an easy chair.

I wonder, if I offer the two a quarter,
Would they leave?

Then I can make out
With the woman of my dreams.

But they look so peaceful and relaxed,
Eating popcorn and watching TV.

Well, maybe next time
They won't be there.

And then I'll kiss my honey
Smack on her lips.

So there!

But why am I going through all this?
I just turned fifty-six!

## What Is It I Seek?

I laid with her,
Not unclad,
Just beside her.
We talked.
We kissed.
We consumed each other
Through the eyes.
We kissed the faces
Many times.

She ravished it, as did I.
She returned my touch.

But I still felt lonely.

Empty …

Then wretched for
Doing that to her,
Though my feelings
Were innocent.

I feel guilty.

The simple thing
Is I don't know who
I want to be with.

She is sweet,
But it is not her.
Maybe I've made my
Choices too many.

Perhaps it is no one
Until that something
I seek reveals itself
And stops lurking
In my periphery.

I pray for this salvation.

## Without My Oldest Son

I am without my oldest son.
He died on November twenty-six, two thousand and none.
Late at night is my guess.
That was when he decided to take a long rest.

He took his life
Nearly in front of me.

I was no more than twenty-five feet away.
The only thing preventing me from seeing
Was slumber, wood, and plaster.

I wish he were here
To tell me of his pain.
He was such a great young guy
Who could've made the world a better place.

I know he was anchored with anger,
Which may have come from somewhere in his childhood.
Or perhaps from the genes it derived.

I wanted to understand and help,
But he made his mind up not to explain
Anything about this somber rain.

I cry a little each and every day
At this great loss.

I loved him so much.
He was my son
Who never said goodbye.
He just left.

## God's Rays

As I pass along the plains, I see clouds ahead.

I watch rain coming down, and
There's lightning just ahead.
Its bolts are magnificent.

It is so wide-open out here.
One can see forever,
Even perhaps the curvature of the earth.

I like that—when I can see
What's all around me,
I even see the weather change.

But mostly, I like the rays
That protrude brilliantly through the clouds.

They make special some field, farm, or town.
It could only be God's anointment
To one of those and everyone else around.

I like it when I can see these miracles take place.
It's all part of God's amazing grace.

He smiles on us like that,
Even when the clouds are dark.

## Radiant Light

The sun breaks through the clouds
In beams of radiant light.

It reigns upon a chosen city, town, or farm.
Those there and around are blessed.

A sign of God's true significance.

## Out on the Plains

I like being out on the plains.
One can see forever all around.

I watch the rain, where it begins and ends!

Sometimes there are lightning bolts
Coming from the sky.
Sometimes on each side.

And then there are the antelope that graze.
It's their home I am in.

Thank you, God.
I am blessed to be here.

## A Flight for God

My darling,
I dream of you tonight
While you are on your flight.

A flight to a distant land
To help others understand
What God is all about.

I know you will be home soon
With great stories to tell.
And perhaps one of someone coming to Christ
To get order in their life.

For that I am anxious to hear
And to see you, my dear.

## One Day on the Plane to Hancock, Michigan (NW FLT 3323)

One day on the plane to Hancock, Michigan,
There was a stewardess named Joan.

She was so pretty
And never in a tizzy.

She walked with such class
And had the best looking ...

Shoes!

She took such great care
Of everyone there.

Her smile was contagious.
Oh, it was outrageous.

I'm so glad
There are people like that.

## I Wonder, I Weep

I loved my son, the one who died.
He didn't have to; he could've survived.

He made a choice in
which I had no voice.

I want to scream out with rage.
He has left me in sort of a cage.

I wonder how and why
he just chose to die.

It hurts deep inside, right at the core.
If I only could have said more …

to him on the night he left.
Perhaps he would still be here.

I cry out in pain.
I think that I am the blame.

But everyone tells me that that is not so.
As he decided the final blow.

Indeed, when he was intent,
did he ever listen to me?

No, he usually never did.
It was Dad's ideas he would rid.

Of course, some he would abide,
unless they broke his stride.

Perhaps it is what he wanted at that moment.
And at this moment, I weep.

### A Beautiful Daughter

I remember her when she was young.
Both of us had so much fun.

She was my first precious child.
About her, I was wild.

We went to breakfast on Saturday mornings.
She always took her time.
And I always ate as if it wouldn't last.

She knew her alphabet from
A to Z.
She won many a spelling bee.

From high school she did graduate.
It was a goal she wouldn't make wait.

She is so special, so unique.

Now she is all grown, a woman of her own.
But somehow, I can't stop looking at her as my little girl.

Remembering those years that I watched her grow
Will always give my heart a very warm glow.

I just love her so.

Dad

## Coffee

Coffee has such a great taste.
I like it in the morning,
Before I go to work.

But now let's see,
What kind do I want?
Hazelnut or gourmet chew?

They ask would I like decaf
Or the stronger brew?

What do you suppose I am to do?
These are far too many questions
After I so early rise.

Can't you just pour me a cup
And let me be surprised?

## At My Son's Grave

People in cars are passing busily by,
Their lives undaunted by my plight.
Trees are swaying in the breeze.
A swishing, pleasant sight.
As I look down and within,
The fresh dirt is not yet settled.
The grass has not grown either
Over my son's grave.

Suddenly, I sense myself
Falling to the ground while
Thrusting my arm deep into the dirt
To open his casket and pull him out.
I shake him, and I brush him off.
And I say, "Wake up!
Wake up now!
Enough of this.
Let's go home!"

## When I Think of You

When I think of you,
I think of beauty
So supreme
It makes my heart glow.

When I think of you,
I think of your love.
To me it does flow.

When I think of you,
It's as if I always knew
That you were the one.

That's what I think when I think of you.

## Pay Those Bills

Pay those bills,
Or they could come out of your will.

Pay those bills.
They never go away.

Yes, yes, you have got to pay.

No one says it's okay,
That you really don't have to pay.

No, no, that they will never say!

You've got to pay those bills, or
They might sell your house!

### If I Could Take a Day Back

If I could take a day back,
I would do it.

"And sir, which day would that be?"
A good question you do ask.

I would make it November 26, two thousand and none.
It was the day my son decided life was no fun.
It was that night that he took his life.

If I had that day, I would talk to him more,
To ask him of his plight, to dissuade him from this act.

I would act in a different way
To take him from his fray.

And if I could, I would love him that much more.

That is the day I would like to take back.

## Propellers' Song

As we are all flying to our homes,
I hear the propellers whirring in tune.

Their whirring goes like this: "We're taking you home.
You're safe with us; no need to make a fuss.
We'll keep on spinning 'round
Til you're all safely on the ground."

### How I Love Thee

How I love thee,
How I cherish thee
With every breath I breathe.

Oh, how I long for thee.
Oh, how I want thee.

Tis beyond my mind and comprehension.

It is your love—that's all.
I guess that is it—that's all.

There is nothing more to explore.

You are my one true love.
I give you my every breath.

## The Airplane Is Tight

The airplane is tight.
We're packed in like
Sardines in a tin.

Still, no one complains.

We all wonder, though—especially since nine one one—
If it's going to be all right.

That nothing can harm
That is out of sight.

We leave ourselves in
God's good hands, and
Pray that his pilots
Are at the helm.

And that we will land safely
To continue to thrive
In our specific realms.

## Clean Slate

As I look beyond the airplane wings on my way home,
I see a vast sea of clouds.

It's as if the earth were all white, and its
Mountains, hills, and rocks were the same.

It's as if we're starting over,
Everyone with a clean slate.

Could it be what God would have us do—
Forgive our neighbors and bid all a, "How do you do"?

## *If the Sky Were White Instead of Blue*

If the sky were white instead of blue,
I would still love you true.

If the moon were not out there,
You know I would still care.

If the leaves were not green in spring,
You would still hear your telephone ring.

And it would be me,
Calling to say

That I love you.

## Don't Get Smart

Don't get smart just because you know how.
Okay, then,
Should I just act stupid?

If I know how to be smart but can't
Because you say

What do I do if the time comes
For me to think?

Should I ask you for help?
You're hardly any help now.
I'm frustrated.

God gave me a brain to use.
The one that you recuse.

I don't know what to do.
Why, I haven't a clue.
Wow, what would I do without you?

### Is This Love?

If you do this,
I'll do that.
Then if you do that,
I'll do this.
Then, honey, if you do this,
I'll do that.
Then when you're finished with this and that,
We can think about doing those.
And I'll love you for that.

## I Touched Him

I touched him,
And he felt cold.

His life spent by,
A twisted cotton sheet.

It seems impossible
That he could not move.

Just hours ago,
He was talking.

I touched him,
And he was cold.

## My Tears Are All Dried Up

My tears are all dried up.
There's nothing left.

I'm going to look for someone else
To fill the void that you left.

Someone who may be like you
So that my heart will be warm to her.

But is that fair to the new love
When it's you that I think of?

My tears are all dried up.
There's nothing left.

## It's a Lonely Time for a Father and a Son

A father who lost a son,
And a son who lost a father

Meet.

A son and father chose to end their lives
With something that could.
Their deaths were untimely, premature.
Neither knew the other or what they were to do.

Why did it happen?
Could we have made a difference?
The haunting questions will remain
As we ponder their plights—as we ponder our own.

Where was God?
Did they call on Him?

Gone are the son and a father who were loved so much.
It has changed our lives forever
As we go on without their presence.

We will never know all the battles that they won
To stay with us and add to the fun.

It's a lonely time for a father and a son

We pray for our Redeemer
To get us through this valley of doubt.

## I Delighted in It

I laid my head back
Into the fold of her bosom.
I felt her so close to me.
I cherished her very flesh.
Her warmth stirred me deep within.
Her sensuality enveloped me.
Her caress melted me through and through.
Her kiss opened my mind and my soul.
And I delighted in it.

I wonder if I will ever
Dream that way again?

## Eighteen

My son, you are still a teenager, but you're not.
You are a young man now, more serious than before.

My heart goes out to you for you will begin many travels.
It is my prayer that on these many journeys,
You will keep our Lord and Savior as your guide.

I love you with all my heart.
And I, too, will always be at your side,
Even though it may only be in memory.

Dad

## His Heart of Gold

There was a man
Named Doofus.
He was a little slow.

Some even said
He was as dumb as a nail.
Others poked fun at him almost every day.

But jabs and jibes never held him back.
He just smiled and said, "Hello."
He treated everyone
With a very warm glow.

He was kind and gentle,
Never thinking of himself.
It was always others he sought to help,
Those less fortunate than himself.

He didn't have any money; it wasn't that.
It was his warmth and love—
That's what made others feel good.

He is gone from us now; he lives no more.
He died in his sleep about a week ago.

Now we wonder—we feel sorrow too—
Why we never gave back
When he always gave us his smile
And his heart of gold.

## My Treasured Love

I long to hold her in my arms,
The treasured love who has gone.

I think of her and days gone by,
And though I don't want to ...

I break down and cry.

I remember those days of laughter—
A little crying too—as we learned of the other.
All about our pasts, the loves we had
And the heartaches too.

I remember quiet dinners, just we two,
Usually by candlelight late in the night.

Her fragrance still lingers on my mind.
That wonderful aroma that is only her.

Her warmth melted my heart.
It embraced me whole.

That was the love just in the past.
The one love that I wanted to last.

Now there seems to be nothing more.
Goodbye, my sweet, my treasured love.

## Love Blooms in All of Us

Love blooms in each of us.
Some more, some less.
Some wild, some caring.
And some just for sex.
But no matter,
Love blooms in all of us.
The question is, which one sustains
And reaches deep within
To let love bloom
Again tomorrow.

## It's Nice to Have Someone

It's nice to have someone
To come home to, to
Talk about the day's events.

Then hold the other
In each other's arms
And kiss as never before.

## Start All Over Again

I once had someone
Who called me honey.
She was a sweet woman
And could even be funny.

Her love for me was strong.
Her touch set me on fire.
Her breath made me melt
And quiver with delight.

Her beauty was astounding.
Her intellect so keen.
I loved her as well
And gave all I could.

But then we both realized
We could go only so far.

Issues in our pasts,
Still unresolved,
Reared their ugly heads.
They made us stall.

It ended for both of us
The way it began,
New strangers who
Thought they could make it last.

Lest for yesterday
That keeps getting in the path.

She is gone now,
No more to return.

I'll have to find another
And start all over again.

Or should I deal first with my past?

## On a Late Friday Afternoon

As late Friday afternoon approaches,

I wonder what I will do, who I can see.
I could go to the gym, get the bod in shape.

Or I can go to a movie and eat popcorn.
Or go to a dance.

With any of these,
I will be among strangers,
People I don't know.

Except for the movies,
I must put on airs.
That same old "All is well. I'm a
Great guy. Why, I'm on top of the world" smile.

It's not that I'm not a great guy; I am
Kind, gentle, and all of that.

It's just that there seems to be no one
To share a little time with
And go beyond just saying hello.

It begins on a late Friday afternoon.

## A Full-Grown Buck

With another year gone,
I'm no longer a fawn.
Why, I'm not even a yearling anymore.
I'm a full-grown buck
Who may have run out of luck.
Every time I turn around,
A new issue/illness has been found.
Perhaps it's my old age
And past transgressions
Catching up.
At any rate, I hope I stick around,
And with some medication,
I should be sound.
I'm not ready to leave this world.
I'd like to finish what I began—
Those things I dreamed of
Before I became a full-grown buck.

## A Father Was a Husband Too

A father was a husband too.

Our mother is all alone.
She loved him true, without reservation.
She longs for his smile and his touch anew.

He loved her without question.
We know that is true.
Why he chose to leave this life
We can only surmise.

A husband was a father too.

A daughter loved him as well.
She cherished his very walk.
She loved to see him when he came home
And to tell him of her day at school.

A son really loved him.
As a father, he taught him much—
When to buy, when to sell,
And when to stay in check until all is well.

Those precious memories
We will cling to no doubt.

Now, though, it is time to go on
As we try and figure this out.
But to do that, we need our Savior
To guide us through this bout.

Please, Lord, let us forgive this husband and father
And be good to ourselves.

(For a friend whose father suicided.)

## I Once Knew a Drunk

I once knew a drunk
With little to give.
He spent half his life
Getting that next drink.

He hustled and screamed
Until he got his way,
Always blaming others for his fray.

It's different with him today.
He has sobered up.
He meets the day.

Now he has something to give,
A bit of his life
To help others make the bid.

Now, drinking is no crime; we all know that.
But for those who get thirstier,
There may be no way back.

This man was lucky; he found God,
Whom he found to be bigger than him.
Now for Him he does trod.

Few make it where this mortal did.
Most die in silence, their life a regret.
Then, acquaintances may sadly say,
"What a wasted legacy they left."

## If Only for Another Day

I sobered up at Arapahoe House,
A place of last resort in Colorado.
It was on April fourteenth
Of nineteen hundred and eighty-seven.

I wanted to do it this time but didn't know how.
After failing so often, my self-esteem was pig chow.

There was a man there much younger than me,
Who was between twenty and twenty-three.
He was bouncing off walls and starting to cry.

He said he saved my life when he pushed me
As a Martian reached for my neck.
He had to push me, don't you see?

Another one, older than me, said without care,
"He comes here to dry out
And be able to eat."

Despite his lifestyle, he looked good for an old man.
He said he couldn't wait to leave.
He wanted to get back on the street,
So he could continue his binge.

While there, I also met an Iranian,
Who seemed as desperate as I
To leave this lonely life behind.
This friend didn't make it.
He had to go out and do it again.

For some reason, I was afraid to do that,
To try it again.
That's when I knew
It was God's love
That told me I didn't need a drink today.

## There and Here

You can never get there from here.
You can always see there,
But when you go there, you're here,
Not there.
There is always in front of you.
Or all around, I guess.
However, no matter what you
Do to get there, you end up here,
Never there.
So how can you ever get there
When you're always here?

## Whatta Crock!

Please don't let me sob.
My masculinity would be robbed.

Let it be rain
That fell from the sky,
Not from my eye.

Oh, please help me cover it up.
All this mist would blow my stuff.

But I have this pain deep inside.
Where do I go to relieve this bind?

This was the bunk that
I learned growing up.

Hide that you're real.
Don't show that you feel.

Whatta crock!

## Scene at a Bar

I saw him at the bar.
It was the very early morn.
I was having breakfast with a friend,
The only place to eat for miles.
Otherwise, I would not have been there.

He wore a trench coat that hung over the seat.
His head covered by a black pullover hat, the kind rappers
Usually wear; he wasn't one of them.
His cold beer, adorned by its label, was just before him.

He peered at its contents in silence,
As if it would tell his future
And let him forget about the past.

The bartender posted at the back
Of the bar, her mind adrift,
Would, with auto response to gesture,
Transform him from a lonely,
Withdrawn person of anguish ...

To that of a happy, serene, and humorous gent
Who would warm her with pseudo-charm and wit.
This eased the time left on her shift.

When he was gone, and her shift was done,
She replaced him on the lonely throne.
It was her turn to put it on.

A sight to study, sad to see.
We finished our breakfast
And left for our day,
Left those lies, pseudo-charm, and wit.

## My Flesh too Might Be Cold

Soon after the shock,
Sorrow, and grief
Over my son's sudden death,
My anger wanted to root in my soul.
Were it not for my Jesus,
My flesh too might be cold.

## My Love Is

My love is like
The most treasured
Of treasures.

She is the awesomeness
Of spring
And the passion of summer.

She is the quietness of fall
And the wonder of winter,
With the new-fallen snow.

My love is all of these.
Into one she does glow.

## We All Wear Uniforms

We all wear uniforms,
Each of us true.
It's a sign of what we represent.
Some are open.
Some are closed.
Still others are near,
A few very far.
But it always tells us
A little about who we are.

### Is It the Way I Learn?

Is it the way I learn,
Hitting my head on every
Brick wall
Till I finally figure it out?

In order to pass through,
It's easier to go around.

## *Face Your Fears*

Face your fears
No matter what they are.

Without doing so,
You'll never go far.

## From This World

I was asleep, yet I heard a noise
Near the front door.

Little did I know that it was my
Son at the end of a twisted sheet.

It was a sound, a sort of choke.
His last gasp of air.

I am troubled by this thought.
Had I realized what it was,

I might have saved him
From himself.

And his escape
From this world.

### It's More than Your Looks

I love the softness
Of your beautiful hair.

Your warm, infectious smile
Is a masterpiece from God.

Your soft, flowing curves
Make me tingle inside.

Ah, but it's more than your looks
That secure my thoughts.

It's also your toes and your mind
That I fondly think of.

I love all of you
With all my heart.

I'll do that for an eternity
And then one more day.

## I Wish I

I wish I could just be what it is I aspire to,
And then I wouldn't have to
Deal with the mental anguish of learning how.

I wish I could just jump off the slopes
Because it's what I want to do,
Without all the training, wearing out muscles.

I wish I could make it all happen on command
Whenever I see it in my mind.

Then I think I'd really have fun.
All the work would never have to be done.

But then wishing about it
Could end up being work too.

Wow! I never thought about that.

## A Time for Us All

There's a time for us all
To reflect on what we've done.

To realize our successes and perhaps our failures tall,
For not all of us will be on top.

Some will be at eternal rest.
Others will not come out of their nest.

Life is for the adventurous, you see.
Those are the ones who will never flee.

And when it is time to reflect,
I'd like to see everyone—

Including myself—as ten feet tall.
And that will be if God is leading the way.

## That Belonged to My Son

That belonged to my son,
The one who died.

All his possessions are in this shoebox.
He's the one who died.

He's not coming back for them.
I'll just keep them for a while.

Then pass them to others,
So his precious memory

Will live on.

## My Silk Lining Rips

Sometimes it's as if
My world is closing in.
I don't know where to turn.
My life seems full of grief.
I look for a blue sky
To get me out of the funk.
Even though it's there,
I'm afraid it won't last
Because it seems
Every time I turn around,
My silk lining rips.

### Talent Can Be Wasted

Talent can be wasted,
That stuff God gave you not to put on a shelf.
So find the talents He has lent you.
Get out there; make something of yourself.
Before you know it, it'll all be gone,
And you'll be left wondering,
What happened, what went wrong?

Going to that cold, lonely pit
Without really knowing who you are,
How far you could've gone
With what He gave you
Would be an empty, lonely way to go.

So please, Lord, help me to know
Just what it is You have for me.
I will fulfill it with You in mind.
Then there will be no cold, lonely pit
Because I'll be ready to come home.

## Change

There's no one to talk to.
Not even me, and I'm you!
I won't listen,
And no one else will either.
I'm tired of hearing about all of
The aches and pains, the heartaches,
The loneliness, and the dashed
Hopes you've had.
Do something: change!

## His Armor Wore Thin

As he grew older,
His armor wore thin.
He was no longer replating it
As he usually did.

Rather, he was starting
To let others get in,
And from this, he began
To experience a new life
From within.
He felt a new freedom
Deep inside, the kind that
Makes you well up and cry.
It's freeing—a great release—
To find out just how much alike
You really are to your fellow man,
Who has been there all the time.

Then one day I heard this friend say,
"I'm sorry I waited so long
To put this armor plate away
And let there be a song."

## Naomi

Now, Naomi is my granddaughter,
A precious sight to see.
She lights up everything inside,
And it shows all over me.

I love it when she touches me
And pats me on the back.
As if to say, "Grandpa, I'm so glad
You're here. I love you so much
I don't want you to leave."

Naomi, my granddaughter,
You've changed my life forever.
For the better, I might add.
But I must confess I'm a little selfish
As I don't want these years
To go by too fast; I want them to last.

Naomi, my precious granddaughter,
I praise your mom and dad
For sharing you with me.
It has filled a lonely void,
One I didn't know I had.

I treasure the moments
I can spend with you,
Just to watch you grow.

And when I leave you,
I think of all the fun we had,
How you warmed my heart and
When I'll get to see you again.

It can't be too soon.
I love you so.

For a friend

## Precious Memories

I remember my little child,
Reaching up with his hand
To touch and play with my face
From the grocery cart he was in.

His hand was soft.
I savored the moment
And hoped it would never end.

I recall other times
When our faces
Were cheek to cheek,
Hugging each other,
Whispering, "I love you,"
While he stood in the crib.

I am blessed to say
All my children did that
Almost every time we were
At the grocery store
And every night
That I tucked them
Into bed.

I praise my Savior
For those precious memories,
The ones I think of now
From my evening chair.

## One Man's Observation

A most pleasing and precious sight
That one can behold is two women
Gleefully conversing in joy and laugher.
The world simply does not exist!

## When the Time Comes

When the time comes,
I hope I'm ready to go,
That my sins will all be forgiven
Before He takes me home.

I guess it's like making sure
All is in order before leaving
On a trip, only this time,
There'll be no coming back.

However, from what the Lord
Has told me, who would want to
Except to visit those
I would miss?

But I'm sure the Lord has already
Thought about all of that.

## As I Lie Back

As I lie back
In my easy chair
To think and
Let time go by,
I'm content to just relax
And let that long-awaited
… … … pass through.
That wondrous tube,
Out, out into the air,
Where nostrils will pretend
They didn't but will wait
For the nauseating odor
To dissipate before
Breathing again.

## I Miss You

I miss the time
We spent together.

Those precious hours
We called our own.

They were quiet.
Oh, so serene.

Then I remember the times
We would talk on and on.

We laughed at ourselves.
How silly we could be!

I cherished those moments—
The love we had.

We knew it would last.

But most of all,
I miss you and your smile.

## Little Girl

Little girl looking at
Her dolls, lost in thought.

What could it be
She is thinking of?

Is it motherhood
Or just what next
Game to play?

Her pretty eyes
Won't say.

## I'm Healing Again

Two years this month—
November 25 to be exact—
My son left this world.
His own desire.

I was healing, getting along,
When friends concerned asked,
"How are you doing; are you okay?"

I know they meant well.
The best, I guess you'd say.

It's just that I would rather
Not have these wounds reappear
And open all the way.

But their questions made me realize
That to open was a choice.
I could reflect on something else—
The other side of his life,
Those good times we had.

I owe these good friends a lot.
They helped me grow,
To see the good side of life,
That side my son and I did have.

I will always love my son.
I know too that he loved me.
I'll remember his smile.
I'm healing again.

## That's as Far as I Ever Got

When I was gonna do it,
That was as far as I ever got.
Those were the old days.
They pass my way a lot.
And even today,
When not careful,
I fall into that same old trap.

Whereupon …

I was always going to do it,
And that's as far as I ever got.

## Another Good Day for an Eagle

Under a crispy blue sky,
Part of the earth was altered, scratched.
Grasses were bent, a few columbines uprooted.

The eagle's wings were magnificent,
Spread over a mule deer carcass,
Roadkill it would have to share.

With its talons set,
This eagle had a tight grip.
Its beak was ripping the flesh.

It was sad and beautiful all the same.
A life gone, a life saved.
Another good day for an eagle.

## When I'm Gone

When I'm gone,
I know you'll lament—
At least for a while.
Then I'd like you
To think of me
As a man who stood
To fight, like most other
Americans, who believed
In this country and wanted
To help others more
Wounded and perhaps
Less dressed than we were.

I always tried to do
What was right—
To stand and put up
An honest, good fight.
At least that's part of
The legacy I hope I
Have left.

Then too, please
Remember those good times
We had—we laughed,
Oh, how we laughed.
I might have pulled
A fast one on you.
Or you got me instead.

I want you to smile.
I would like you to laugh.
I hope you burst out in a cheer
Because that's what
Your friendship, your warmth,
And your love did for me.

Now, you may think my last
Battle has been lost.
Ah, but it's victory instead.

My precious Savior called me home.

## The Lord Gave Me a Fine Brain

The Lord gave me a fine brain.
But oftentimes
I'm too stubborn
To use it.

### It's Always about a Love I Once Had

It's always
About a love
I once had.
Times gone by;
They are no more.

It escapes me,
After a while just
How I always end up
Without the one
I truly loved.

It's always about a love I once had.

## I Love Holding You

You are the one
I have sweet dreams of.

You are the precious
Thoughts of my day.

You are the giddy
Thoughts of my night.

You are always on my mind.
I love that.

But not as much
As I love holding you.

### The Struggles We Have

The struggles we have
Can form us strong.

If we stay the course,
We win the song.

But not alone do we
Need to trod through

This agony long because—

Remembering from
Whence we came.

Our Lord and our prayers
Will make this way.

Thus, fear and darkness
Are cast away.

## In Between the Doors

There was a time,
So simple it seems,
When lilacs bloomed,
And roses were bright red.

Now, though, it's all changed.
They are no more.
At least not just now
In between doors.

## No Calls at Home

Often as I open the
Front door to my home,
I wonder if there's a
Call from a friend.
But then I remember, I don't have
A phone; I only use a cell,
And it's with me.
There are no calls.
Oh well, maybe later
Someone will think of me.
Perhaps even a bill collector,
And I'll get to say hello!

## There Will Be Another Day

There will be another day
That I will love.

For now, though,
It's sorrow that I feel.

A sad ending to some,
Wonderful fun.

Neither of us wanting
To talk about what went wrong.

There was love.
There was affection.

Until we got too close,
Close enough to know

Who the other really was,
Or was not.

Then it's one or the
Other who set in motion

The seeds of destruction
Of a beautiful love.

And when I'm healed,
There will be another love.

## Which Eye?

They are wonderful
People, the ones
With the funny eyes.
I just wish they'd
Tell me which one
To look at.

But then,
They may not
Want to.
It may be a bit
Of parity; I believe
I've seen a smile
On their faces
As they've
Witnessed this dilemma!

## One Is Always Someone's

Toward spring,
Trees prepare anew.
Old leaves have
Already dropped off.
Stubborn old branches
Graceful one day finally
Look to rest, while
Each is remembered
For a unique day.

The young—the new ones—
Are anxious to bud,
To take on the breezes.
It's one of the seasons;
Always there is a season.
Four times strong,
And one is always
Someone's.

## It's at Angles that He Lives

Today is his birthday.
He would have been twenty-three.
He decided not to celebrate
A year ago and eleven.
He's gone from us forever,
Never to be seen again; except
At times in others he returns.
It's then, at different angles, that he lives.

Otherwise, he's gone,
And it's only his memory that lives.

## Come Here and Love Me

Come here and love me.
I need you tonight.

I don't want to be alone.
I can't bear you out of my sight.

Come here and love me.
I need you tonight.

Throw your arms around me,
And squeeze me real tight.

Tell me that you love me
And that you are mine.

Come here and love me.
I need you tonight.

## The Sky

How beautiful is the sky?
So clear and blue.
Sometimes white with fluff
To give it a hue.
I love that clear-blue sky.
So wondrous and surreal.
It's something I take for granted
Whenever I start my day.

## I Wonder about My Love

I wonder about my love
As she travels far away.
I wonder if she thinks of me
In a very special way.
Will she come back
And love me just as true?
Or has she found another
Whom she'll visit again real soon?

## I Love It

I love the way
You say, "Come here."

And I love it when you
Touch my flesh.

And I especially love it
When you say,

"I love you, sweetheart."

## Sleep

To sleep is to delight
In dream and tranquility.
It is a time to relax the torso,
The limbs, the mind,
The soul, the teeth,
And the eyes.

It is a time to wander
To places we can't go,
Or that would be
Considered delusions in day.

It is a time I'd like to know.

### Sleep Escapes Me Again!

It's another of those nights
When the chemicals within
Lack effect for the tiredness without.
The eyes droop, the lids hang,
The arms are limp.
The legs struggle to stand.
It's even hard to close the mouth.
You'd think I'd just pass out,
But sleep escapes me again.
It escapes me again!
Just when I need it most,
It escapes me again ...

## On Loneliness and Love

It's lonely.
Even among you,
There's a void inside
That yearns for more.
It doesn't matter
Where I am.

It doesn't change.
That special
Someone is missing.

I long for that caress.
I desire that touch.
I need that precious
Exchange of minds.

Most of all,
I want to love
Just her.

## God Gives Answers and Tools, so You Better Be Ready!

I am in the thick of it.
Right in the middle,
You might say.
It doesn't feel too good,
But I did ask God what I
Should do, and I suppose
This was His answer.
And now I have
These tools to get the job done.
Only doing it isn't any fun.

I'm more accustomed to procrastinating,
Dreaming, and otherwise
Just chatting about it.
Really not getting it done.
After all that is/was
My comfort zone.
Why, it would be easier to
Just sit on my bun!

## A Busy Love

I hunger for love,
But I don't have time.
I'm too busy
With nothing really.
I'm spending my time
Putting out fires—
One here, one there.
Hustling all the time
If not for someone else,
Then it's to cover my tush.
There is just no time
For the love I hunger for.

The love I want in my life.

Do you suppose
I could schedule
Something like a
Busy lunch

With someone as busy as I?

Then perhaps a busy dinner
And then a busy movie.
Then we might develop
A busy love,
And then neither of us
Would be lonely.

Why, we could have
The perfect busy love.

Not!

### I Want to Wait for Her Love

I want to wait for her love.
I really do.

Just for that right one
To brighten the portal of my heart.

But in the meantime,
What do I do?

## Waiting for Water on the Farm

Down by the dam
On our farm,
I used to like watching
The cows and horses
Go for water each day.
They would mosey
Down to this watering hole,
Always the cows first.
Dan and Kate, the horses,
Had to wait.

The cows took their
Sweet ole time filling
Up those four bellies.
Then before leaving,
They'd always drop
A few of those pies
Then meander
Off in their slow, arrogant style.

I watched ole Dan and Kate,
Waiting for their tastes.
They'd kick their hooves at the ground
And neigh with discontent.

I couldn't help but wonder

If they might be telling
Those cows to hurry up,
Else they'd get a hoof
Where it might make
Their milk taste
Kind of funny.

But the cows never seemed to care.

(More of the stories from dad that he asked me to write
about the farm where he grew up near Chassell, Michigan.)

## Dan and Kate

Dan and Kate were our horses
That worked hard
On our farm.

Now and then, Kate could be stubborn.
I'd have to tap her on the rump.
It'd get her in the
Mood to till the field
From morning to about noon.

She was still a good horse.
I liked her a lot.

Now Dan was different.
He was always raring
To go; he was ready at morning
And would work all day long.

He was a good horse,
And I liked him a lot too.

The two got along well.
I think Dan kept Kate in line.
I think he talked to her
While they were eating
Their oats and hay.

I think of those horses—Dan and Kate—
With fondness today, although
It's been about seventy-five years
Since I last saw them around here.

(Another story Dad remembered when
I asked him about the old farm in
Chassell, Michigan.)

## Build from the Past

Now is not the time
To lament
Over things past and gone.

How many times
I have heard and said
That sort of phrase.
So old, so understood,
Still, so barely worn.

Now, though, is the time to live
And build from the past
I already built.

### The Kids Are All Grown

The kids are all grown,
None of them wrong.
Grown from differences,
Families or none,
It doesn't matter.
They grew up.
At least most
Had that chance.

They used tools that
Parents, someone, or others,
Gave them to make
The best of their days.
Yes, and some of it
Worked, and some … hey!

We did what we could
With what we had.
For some of us,
It was very little.
For others, quite
A lot.

## I Would've Liked Him to Be Here

In November, it'll be three,
Three years ago that he left.
I was just there today
To visit him, talk over him.

I know he didn't hear me.
It made me weep, sob; I miss him.
I feel weak from it; it drained me.
But I had to go, get as close as I could.

It's Father's Day today.

I would've liked him to be here
With his sister and brother and me.

## I Lay with Her

I lay with her,
Not unclad,
Next to her.

I kissed her cheek.
I kissed her nose.
I kissed her ear.
I kissed her forehead.
I kissed her eyelids gently
And her smile
Many times.

She lavished in it as did I.
She kissed me
Like that.

Her sensuality and
Flesh aroused me,
As mine did her.

She whispered that to me.

We let ourselves be
For the moment.

Reveling in the spirit,
The newness,
The purity
Of each other's love.

## God Called Him Home

God called him home
Much before his time.
He was too young to go.

He was my brother.

God didn't need him.
Why then would He take him?

I miss him!
I want him back!

I dreamt one night
I went to heaven to get him
To take him home.
I spoke with God and told Him so.
He was kind; well, He was God, and He
Said, "My dear, you can take
Him if you wish. I'll let him go, but
His safety and welfare are in your hands.
You'll be responsible."

I stopped; I, I wanted my brother back.
My heart pounded—oh, no; oh, no.
What if I …

Then I awoke.

Thank You, Lord, for loving me
And for loving the one I've missed.

(For a friend.)

## Unlock the Door to My Heart

I wanted to love once.
I suppose I still do.

I just can't seem to
Find that precious someone

Who'll put the light on
So I can find the key.

To unlock the door,
The one to my heart.

The one I've kept locked
So no one would get in.

## The Aurora Only You Could Bring

When I think of you,
My flesh peaks;
My desires accentuate.

You are the Venus,
Voluptuous essence
And purity of thought.

I am enraptured by the brilliance
Of your eyes, your radiating smile,
And the aurora only you could bring.

You have devoured
My being and encapsulated
My mind and soul.

My spirit has been freed
To love again
And trust in what that may bring.

## Don Juan Wannabe

I don't understand
How you think
From that tiny
Blob atop your spine
That you believe
Yourself to be
That essential chocolate
That always turns a woman on,
Making her feel as if she's
Been clubbed into a delirious mist—
A delirium of love—
When she really
Feels as if she'd just been
Spayed!

Wake up, you fool,
Wake up!

## I Thought I Loved

I have loved
Many times,
This is true.
At least I
Thought I had.
Love comes and goes,
Not one for too long.
The thrill, the frown—
Has love eluded me?

Here I am again, all alone.
Or is it me
Who has eluded love
By finding a way
To leave the one love
I thought I loved.

## When I Choose

When I choose,
I chose.
When I don't,
I didn't.

Isn't that it?

Either way, I act.
Either way, I go.
I could be right;
I could be wrong.

Just right or wrong,
Only right or wrong,
Not in between.

But I've learned.

On most matters,
It really
Doesn't matter.
What matters ...

Is that you choose.

## When It's Time to Sing

When it's time to sing,
It doesn't matter when.
It only matters that you're ready.
When you hear the ring,
Your time is then.
It's your tune, time to bloom.
Unless, of course,
You already know.
Then it's my hope
That you're already in bloom.

### I'll Never Understand

God is our guide.
Jesus, so kind.

Why He loves me
I'll never understand.

All I know is that He died for my sins.
If that isn't love, you tell me what is.

## Nothing Brings Him Back

I have begged.
I have pleaded.

I have bargained.
I have offered myself in his place.

Nothing brings him back—nothing.
He stays where he is.

I have asked for forgiveness
If I had done him wrong.

I regret scolding him the night he left.

I have begged leniency
From both him and God.

Yet he doesn't come back
From under the dirt.

His soul is in heaven,
His body underground.

Something he chose,
Something I lost.

He was my son.

## There Is a Time

There is a time
To know each other.

There is a time
To love with passion.

There is a time
To tend to dreams.

There is a time
To say goodbye.

There was a time
For all those things.

## My Darling

I cherish the thought
That you have chosen
To love me.

But most of all,
It is I who am blessed
To have had the chance
To love you.

## Bumblebee

What side are you on,
Bumblebee?

You buzz around me,
Checking things out.

Go, go away!
Shoo, you bumblebee.

Find someone else's other side.

## This Day Is Precious

Release me from
The bonds of morn.
I must awaken
To face the dawn.
This day is precious.
There is no more,
And what was is gone.

### An Earlier Time

A vast sea of clouds,
So pearly and white,
Remind me of a time
When I was a virgin.
Why, I was an innocent lad.

Now times are older,
With much under the belt.
I have asked for forgiveness
To get nearly back
What has been already dispensed.

## Night Flight

I can't see the clouds anymore.
The embers have died.

Blackness it is.

I can't even see the sky.
It's a cold feeling.

I don't want to go that way!

I should close my eyes.
Pray.

Believe in the Pilot.
Follow Him.

Let Him
Take me home
With the pilot He chose.

## Days Gone By

I think of days gone.
Why, I do not know.

Perhaps it's just the age;
Reflection is in style.

I recall my youth,
My middle too.

Now it's the senior time,
A time to reflect on days gone by.

In the midst of lots of things to do.

## Alone

Tonight, as I bask
In the bulb
Of this old room,
It's hard to envision
Not being alone
The rest of my life.

## Cursing Again

It's Sunday morning.
Time to get up.
It's the Lord's Day, or
So we've made it that way.
I'll go to His place,
Worship His name,
And then be back
On the streets, probably
Cursing again.

Lord, what are You
Going to do with me?

## How Do You Say Goodbye?

How do you say goodbye
To those you love and cheer?

The answer is simple; you don't.
You just keep them in your heart.

## He May Have Called Me

I have been everywhere
There is to go.
Oh, I'm sure there are
A few places that I would've
Liked to have gone,
Only I can't think of where just now.

I have been blessed
With a family—children, one who is far—who love me as I am,
Friends who have been with me all along,
And a wife who has been at my side;
I feel as though I've known her all my life.

These are the things I wished for
In my early days.
God gave them graciously.
He has let me delight in them.
He has let me love them,
Especially my wife.
He showed me how.

And now, it seems
It is my time … my time.

He may have called me.
I don't know why.
He just has—
Unless He changes His mind.

I don't want to leave.
I don't want to go.
I don't want to miss anyone.

But soon, I guess, I may see Him.
I'll be in my Father's home.

That my loved ones
Will be the ultimate blessing!

Know that.

(For a friend.)

## When Summer Comes

When summer comes,
My love will be there.

When summer comes,
I'll hold her in my arms.

When summer comes,
I'll kiss her lips.

Summer with my love
Is every day of the year.

### I've Lost Too Many

I don't feel like
Writing poems
About dead sons
Anymore.

My heart is not in it.
It never was!

I've lost too many.
Two sons—all I had.

Both long before their times—
At least in my mind.
They should still be here
To till the life they chose.

### I Want to Say, "I Love You"

I want to say,
"I love you,"
To that special someone.
But it can't be
Just anyone.
It must be you.

## I'm not Really Out with You

I'm out with you.
But I'm not really
Out with you.

My heart yearns
Elsewhere; where
I do not know.

I have no one
In particular.
Oh, perhaps
One or two.

But we have
Had our day.
It wouldn't work
With either,
I'm afraid.

There are others
In my periphery,
But not ones with
Whom I would stay.
They're just there.

I'm out with you,
But not really out
With you.

I am sorry for
Wasting your time.

Forgive me.

## A Man and a Woman

A man and a woman
Belong with each other.
God planned it that way.
Not for others.

### She Felt as Empty as He

She was out with him,
A date.
But he wasn't out with her.
He was there,
But he was elsewhere.
She didn't know
That he wasn't there
Except for his gaze
Now and then.

It was hard for him to hide.

Then she knew
And felt as empty as he.

## Essence

Love between us,
It's the essence of life.
The adhesion
Of two into one,
A man and a woman.

## Love

It's not often when you meet
Someone who stirs
You deep within.
It is then the time
To flee from fright,
That thing that I just felt.
It feels as though I have
Known you
For longer than that moment.
Perhaps it was just the
Camaraderie of our years.
Perhaps not.
But that aside,
It feels so good
That I again
Tingle inside.

## Scott in My Memory

It has been almost a year
Since my son flew beyond
The sun to heaven,
To our Father's home.

I miss him terribly.

He would have been
Twenty-one on the next Friday,
The one after tomorrow.

My heart still aches as I
Lament his passing
As the day nears when he did.

With the healing there is
Still the pain; it's getting better.

The good news is that I had
Nearly twenty years to love him and
Those years for him to love me.

Those are great memories.
A few snarls at times, but so it
Goes, raising a child; it's expected.
They are, after all, growing up,
God's precious gifts to us.

He loved God, photography, his mother,
His father, sister, and brother, and
He loved all his friends.

His name was Scott, and he
Was beautiful!

Printed in the United States
By Bookmasters